HEADLINE SERIES

No. 302   FOREIGN POLICY ASSOCIATION   Spring

Global Population Growth:
21st Century Challenges

by George D. Moffett

Cover Design: Bob Mansfield $5.95

#31003049

The Author

GEORGE D. MOFFETT, who holds a Ph.D. in history from George Washington University, is a diplomatic correspondent for *The Christian Science Monitor,* where his series on global population earned the Population Institute's 1992 Global Media Award. He has been a visiting scholar at the Center for International Affairs at Harvard University and at the Woodrow Wilson International Center for Scholars, where this book was written. He served in the Carter White House as an assistant to the chief of staff.

Financial support for *Critical Masses,* from which this book is excerpted, was provided by the Rockefeller Foundation and the Charles Stewart Mott Foundation.

The Foreign Policy Association

The Foreign Policy Association is a private, nonprofit, nonpartisan educational organization. Its purpose is to stimulate wider interest and more effective participation in, and greater understanding of, world affairs among American citizens. Among its activities is the continuous publication, dating from 1935, of the HEADLINE SERIES. The author is responsible for factual accuracy and for the views expressed. FPA itself takes no position on issues of U.S. foreign policy.

HEADLINE SERIES (ISSN 0017-8780) is published four times a year, Spring, Summer, Fall and Winter, by the Foreign Policy Association, Inc., 729 Seventh Ave., New York, N.Y. 10019. Chairman, Paul B. Ford; President, John Temple Swing; Editor in Chief, Nancy L. Hoepli; Senior Editors, Ann R. Monjo and K.M. Rohan. Subscription rates, $20.00 for 4 issues; $35.00 for 8 issues; $50.00 for 12 issues. Single copy price $5.95; double issue $11.25. Discount 25% on 10 to 99 copies; 30% on 100 to 499; 35% on 500 and over. Payment must accompany all orders. Postage and handling: $2.50 for first copy; $.50 each additional copy. Second-class postage paid at New York, N.Y., and additional mailing offices. POSTMASTER: Send address changes to HEADLINE SERIES, Foreign Policy Association, 729 Seventh Ave., New York, N.Y. 10019. Copyright 1994 by Foreign Policy Association, Inc. Design by K.M. Rohan. Printed at Science Press, Ephrata, Pennsylvania. Spring 1993. Published July 1994.

Library of Congress Catalog Card No. 94-71669
ISBN 0-87124-158-7

1

Rapid Population Growth ~ Truths and Consequences

More than most people realize, the subject of population growth and its consequences is immensely complex and highly nuanced, the more so because the field of population studies lies at the intersection of so many different disciplines. Beyond the nuances, there are the minefields. The issue of global population is intensely controversial. This should come as no surprise since, in one way or another, it touches virtually every aspect of the human experience, from the intimate to the cosmic. Mighty debates rage among experts over whether economic underdevelopment is the cause or consequence of rapid population growth; whether family planning or economic and social development is the best way to slow population growth; whether population growth is a crisis or a blessing in disguise; whether forests and croplands, fisheries and the earth's atmosphere are on the verge of destruction, and, if so, whether population growth plays a role. No one can be entirely neutral when dealing with such provocative issues. But even though the author's own biases may be evident in the pages that follow, the book is not intended as a piece of special pleading. On the contrary, its primary purpose is to define the large measure of common ground that exists among experts with respect to two critical points—points that policymakers, above all, need to understand.

The first concerns what *needs* to be done: However sharply they may disagree about the long-term implications of rapid population growth, the vast majority of experts believe that any prudent strategy for dealing with the future must include measures to slow projected population growth. The second point concerns what *can* be done: Despite disagreements over tactics, broad strategic agreement exists among population experts that slowing population growth requires a combination of effective family planning and development plans that include, but are not limited to, increased educational opportunities for girls. If both of these steps were taken with dispatch, the population problem could be solved within the lifetime of today's children.

Because the poverty and environmental degradation to which rapid population growth has contributed are so unpleasant to come face-to-face with; because the population issue is too often presented as a statistical rather than a deeply personal matter; because long-term demographic trends are often underreported in a media environment in which breaking or sensational news is favored—for all of these reasons there is a high level of public ignorance about the population problem and thus there is little pressure on policymakers to move it to the top of the agenda, where it belongs.

There are three reasons why breaking through the barriers of misinformation and apathy are especially crucial now. The first is that population growth is one of the global problems that will bear most heavily on the peace and prosperity of the international system during the next few decades. The second is that the end of the cold war offers an unprecedented opportunity for policymakers to accelerate the dramatic progress that has already been made during the past three decades in reducing global birthrates. The third is that unless policymakers seize that opportunity during the decade of the 1990s, it will be far harder in the next century to stabilize population growth at a sustainable level. It is largely to call attention to this opportunity and to point to the consensus for action that already exists that this book has been written.

Population Curve

Through most of human history the world's population remained below 300 million, capped by birthrates and death rates that were locked in a seemingly permanent equilibrium. But sometime after the year 1600, the line demographers use on graphs to plot population growth began to stir, and then took an unexpected—and until now, permanent—turn upward. The ascent was slow at first. The line probably crossed the half-billion mark sometime during the seventeenth century. Nudged along by improvements in agriculture and public health, and then by the Industrial Revolution, it climbed higher through the eighteenth century. After the turn of the nineteenth century it reached a milestone, passing the one-billion mark for the first time in human history. That was around the year 1800, not long after the English economist Thomas Malthus penned his famous essay warning that such growth would outpace food supplies and hold mankind in the grip of poverty.

The line continued upward into the present century and began its steepest ascent in the years after World War II, when two developments sent death rates plummeting in the poor nations of Asia, Africa and Latin America. One was the introduction of antibiotics and the advent of public-health programs that led to mass immunizations and improvements in sanitation and water supplies. The other was an agricultural revolution based on chemical fertilizers, irrigation and improved seed strains that dramatically expanded food supplies. The combined effect was to reduce mortality rates. But with no corresponding drop in birthrates, the population line was propelled into the demographic stratosphere.

By the 1960s the *rate* of population growth reached 2.1 percent globally and 2.5 percent among developing countries—the highest ever recorded—and then dropped off. But, driven by the disproportionately large percentage of young people in the nations of the Third World, the line plotting the *actual growth in human numbers* continued its upward course. Several decades of the fastest population growth in human history still lie ahead, according to the United Nations. If fertility declines fast enough, the line will level off sometime after the middle of the twenty-first century. If it does not, its ascent will continue into the twenty-second. Its long upward journey will then, finally, be at an end.

Over the years demographers have groped for ways to convey some sense of what this extraordinary growth in human numbers means. The sheer speed of population growth is suggested by this simple comparison: It took 18 centuries from the time of Christ for the earth to reach its first one billion inhabitants, but only *one century* to reach its second and only *one decade* to reach its latest billion. Or by this projection: Ninety-six hours from now the earth will have one million more inhabitants, which translates into (at 1990 population levels) a new Pittsburgh or Boston every two days, a new Germany every eight months, a new Mexico or two new Canadas every year, a new Africa and Latin America *combined* during the decade of the 1990s alone. Today's net daily global population increase is 250,000.

The world's population now stands at about 5.6 billion, on its way to 6 billion by the turn of the century. At current growth rates it will double by the year 2035, while in Africa, where growth rates remain the highest in the world, population will double in just over half that time, from 670 million today to 1.4 billion by about 2015. Exactly when and at what level global population growth will finally peak is extremely difficult for demographers to predict. The precondition to an eventual leveling off is getting "fertility"—that is, the average number of children a woman has during her reproductive years—down to "replacement" level, or the two children a couple needs to replace itself. Not counting China, which has a fifth of the world's population and its most aggressive program to curb birthrates, fertility in the developing countries averages 4.4 children per family.

One problem that makes the task of projecting ultimate population levels so difficult is that even if replacement fertility were reached overnight, it would be years before the world's population would stop growing, mainly because of a phenomenon called population momentum. About 40 percent of the population of developing countries

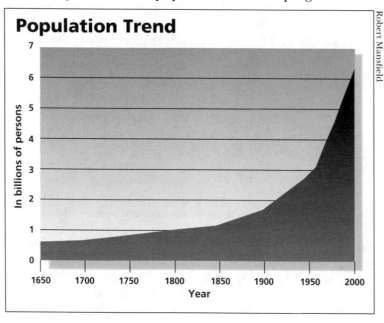

is under the age of 15. With so many just entering their reproductive years, population is destined to increase for decades more. If Mexico, for example, were instantly to achieve replacement fertility, its population would still double over the next 50 years. Japan, which attained replacement fertility in 1957, will not reach zero population growth until 2006. Thus, as demographers analogize, stopping population growth is like stopping a speeding train: There is a long delay between putting on the brakes and coming to a full halt.

The range of theoretically possible population futures is suggested by the UN, whose periodic projections have long been a standard reference point for demographers. If fertility declines to replacement level immediately, population could level off at around 8.5 billion by the middle of the next century. Under the UN's 1992 medium projection—the number regarded as the most probable maximum—population would reach 10 billion around the year 2050 and peak sometime during the twenty-second century at about 11.5 billion. The projection is based on educated guesses that replacement fertility will kick in at different times in different countries or regions: by 2030 in India, for example, but not until 2050 in Africa.

Demographers explain that developing nations like Nigeria are just at the beginning of a four-stage demographic transition that most of the countries of Western Europe and North America began in the nineteenth century and completed several decades ago. Stage one begins in preindustrial societies, where both birthrates and death rates are high, producing the kind of population stability that characterized much of human history before the seventeenth century. In the second stage of the transition, improved living conditions, sometimes produced by industrialization, reduce death rates, but birthrates remain high because children are still needed in premodern rural societies to provide farm labor and eventual old-age security for their parents. In stage two, the benefits of having children continue to outweigh the costs. In the third stage of the transition, improved living conditions, urbanization and the upgrading of the status of women reverse the calculus of childbearing. As a family's dependence on children decreases and as the need to educate children increases, the cost of rearing children begins to outweigh the benefits, producing a desire for smaller families. In the final stage, a new parity is attained between low birthrates and death rates, which once again produces population stabilization, though at a much higher level of population.

Contraceptive Revolution

Thanks to economic growth and comprehensive family-planning programs, a small number of developing nations—Thailand and South Korea, for example—have already completed the transition, nearing or reaching replacement fertility in a few short decades. Many more, including a number of Latin American countries, are progressing through stage three. But another group of nations, mostly African, lingers in the perilous realm of stage two, where declines in birthrates trail declines in death rates. Some demographers are worried that without the impetus of industrialization and economic development, the factors that helped lower birthrates in Europe and East Asia, the poorest countries could get stuck at stage two, with catastrophic results.

Fortunately, one development is likely to minimize the prospect that developing countries will fall into this "demographic trap": the contraceptive revolution that began sweeping the developing world in the late 1960s and extended family-planning services into the remotest corners of the globe. The conventional wisdom has long been that, because it spurs urbanization, reduces dependence on children, and creates opportunities for women outside the home, economic development is the best and perhaps only contraceptive. It was a logical assumption, since it was based on the European and North American experience.

But the extension of family-planning programs has made an independent contribution to reducing the birthrates, usually in tandem with social and economic development, as in East Asia, but occasionally alone, as in the case of Bangladesh.

Bangladesh is one of the poorest and most densely populated nations on earth, where a rural lifestyle still makes large families a logical choice. Even so, two decades after the government and various private organizations began aggressively promoting modern contraceptives, fertility has declined from 7 to 4.9 children per family, while contraceptive use has risen from 3 percent of women of reproductive age to over 40 percent. Under the more controlled conditions produced in the Matlab region of southern Bangladesh, where infusions of outside aid have sustained a large experimental program, contraceptive prevalence now exceeds 60 percent.

In Bangladesh and elsewhere, researchers have found that family-planning programs have not only helped to satisfy the demand for contraceptives needed to space pregnancies and limit family size but, by legitimizing the idea of smaller families, have actually created new demand.

A further variable that could affect population projections is the AIDS (acquired immune deficiency syndrome) pandemic, the impact of which has been greatest in regions of the world where the fastest population growth is occurring. According to the World Health Organization (WHO), 40 million people worldwide may be infected with HIV (human immunodeficiency virus) by the turn of the century. Some two thirds of AIDS cases are believed to be concentrated in sub-Saharan Africa, with HIV prevalence estimated at nearly 25 percent among adults in urban areas in the worst-hit countries, including Uganda, Zaire and Tanzania. The epidemic will take its heaviest toll among infants and among young adults in their prime productive and reproductive years.

Most demographers doubt that AIDS will lead to negative population growth since birthrates still far exceed current and projected AIDS death rates in even the worst-affected countries. "The view held by some people that 'AIDS will take care of the population problem' is completely erroneous," one group of experts concluded in 1993. At the same time, experts are worried that the AIDS epidemic could hasten the spread of other diseases, including tuberculosis, and thereby increase death rates. A more pervasive worry is that crowded and unsanitary conditions, to which rapid population growth has contributed, could provide a hothouse environment for the spread of antibiotic-resistant strains of other infectious diseases.

AIDS Education Could Slow Growth

Paradoxically, the AIDS cloud that hangs heaviest over Africa and South and Southeast Asia could have a silver lining. If AIDS education succeeds in convincing large numbers of adults to limit the number of their sexual partners and to use condoms regularly, the result could be a decrease not only in HIV infections but in population growth.

Behind the stark reality that the world's population now surges by 11,000 people every hour of every day, there are hopeful considerations. One is that the astronomical population growth that has occurred since the start of the seventeenth century is a historical anomaly and not, as one UN study notes, a natural, normal or, in all likelihood, permanent feature of human history. The factors that caused it are unlikely to be repeated, since gains in development, public health, women's rights and contraceptive technology are likely to bring four centuries of accelerating growth in human numbers to a gradual end. The runaway population growth of the past several centuries is thus a unique chapter in demographic history. Most experts believe that it will end sometime late in the twenty-first or early twenty-second century when one of two possible states is reached. One is a new balance in the world as a whole between births and deaths, stabilizing global population for the first time in over four centuries. The other is more likely and less tidy: a continuation of differential growth rates, with population declining in most areas while still growing, though at slower rates, in others.

Another heartening fact is that because of the combination of family-planning programs and improving economic conditions that exists in many developing nations, the demographic transition that took a century to achieve in the West has been telescoped in much of the developing world. The circumstances that have enabled countries like Thailand to reach replacement fertility within a mere generation are likely to be duplicated in other countries as information on how to manage successful family-planning programs is more widely disseminated and as command economies give way to free-market systems and thus to the faster economic development that will hasten the transition to lower fertility.

Some economists have also taken heart from the fact that the biggest population explosion in history is occurring in the context of the most sweeping technological changes, changes that could well mitigate the worst effects of population growth. The communications revolution has extended the reach of family-planning messages into the homes of vast numbers of Third World poor, legitimizing the small-family norm and influencing family-size preference. Agricultural technologies have revolutionized farm production, resulting in quantum leaps in output. A combination of market mechanisms, conservation and substitution techniques has stretched available supplies of mineral resources despite unparalleled increases in population. Combined with intelligent public policies, these economists argue, technologies that can expand freshwater supplies, reduce atmospheric pollution, or coax more food from fixed quantities of arable land can make the concept of limits obsolete, no matter what the ultimate size of the earth's population.

But when it comes to weighing a future that will have to

accommodate double or triple the world's present population, even with the family-planning revolution, caution should outweigh optimism. To understand the reasons why, consider that in most of sub-Saharan Africa the demographic transition has barely begun, much less progressed toward replacement fertility. Despite notable increases in contraceptive prevalence and decreases in fertility in a few African nations, the continent as a whole is an anchor that the rest of the world is dragging on its voyage toward population stabilization. Or consider that some of the nations long heralded as family-planning success stories have faltered on the road to replacement fertility. In India, the country that launched the family-planning revolution, but which has been anything *but* a success story, fertility has plateaued at just under four children per family. As a result, India could well overtake China as the world's most populous nation before the middle of the next century.

Growth Rates Highest in Poorest Regions

Temporary stalls have been recorded in other countries, with huge numerical consequences. Even though fertility has dropped off sharply in Indonesia since the early 1960s, to three children per couple, its population is still growing at an annual rate of 1.7 percent. In the unlikely event that it remains that high, the country with the most successful family-planning program in the Islamic world will be twice its current size of 188 million in a mere 42 years. In all, 63 countries with a total of 850 million people still average more than five children per family.

The main reason so many demographers are worried is that population growth is concentrated in the very regions of the world least able to cope with it. Ninety-five percent of future population growth will occur in the developing nations, where three of every four people now live and where nine tenths of humanity will live in the near future. And most of them will live in the most vulnerable areas of the developing world: cities. It is not this skewed distribution alone that concerns many experts but the breakneck speed with which population growth is likely to take place, a speed so far out of balance with rates of economic and social advancement that it imposes heavy penalties on nations and families alike.

It is hard to imagine that governments in at least some developing nations will not be taxed to or beyond what they can bear just to keep up with the relentless demands such fast-growing populations will make on jobs and housing and social services. Difficult economic conditions, exacerbated by rapid population growth, have already prompted millions of rural poor to migrate to cities and millions more—at a rate of 10,000 per day, according to the UN High Commissioner for Refugees—to cross international borders in search of a better life. Those who stay behind will press upon surrounding farmland and intensify pressure on ecological systems.

"The problem is not population growth per se," explains Bruce Wilcox, a biologist who heads the Institute for Sustainable Development in Menlo Park, California. "It's when the rate of population growth exceeds the rate at which technology and social change can compensate. When that happens, the result is environmental damage and human suffering. The real issue is thus not whether Earth can sustain 10 billion people or 100 billion people, but how much damage will be done between now and when humanity comes to terms with the constraints of the global environment."

Although many experts believe that rapid population growth is a root cause of economic underdevelopment, political instability and environmental degradation, the population issue has not evoked much public concern in the United States since the late 1960s and early 1970s, when books like Paul Ehrlich's *The Population Bomb* and *The Limits to Growth,* based on a study sponsored by the international Club of Rome, created a stir with projections of famine and economic collapse. Nor, curiously, has it

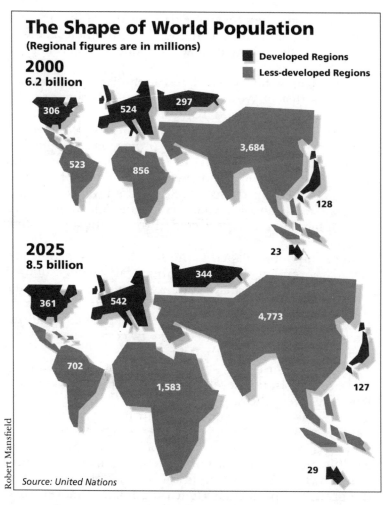

The Shape of World Population
(Regional figures are in millions)

■ Developed Regions
■ Less-developed Regions

2000
6.2 billion

306
524
297
3,684
523
856
128
23

2025
8.5 billion

344
361
542
4,773
702
1,583
127
29

Robert Mansfield

Source: United Nations

assumed among recent American policymakers the kind of
priority given to it by one secretary of state in the 1960s,
Dean Rusk, who warned that getting nuclear weapons and
high global population growth rates under control were
the two greatest challenges facing mankind. But neither
ignorance nor apathy will spare Western nations from the

implications of the growing body of evidence that population growth, alone or in conjunction with other factors, is having significant and adverse consequences, and not just in poor nations.

In the United States, which has a population growth rate five times that of Western Europe and four times that of Japan, immigration and natural population growth are occurring so fast that the U.S. Census Bureau was recently forced to revamp its long-term projections. In the late 1980s the bureau projected that the U.S. population would peak at just over 300 million before the middle of the next century. New projections issued just four years later put the 2050 total at between 383 million and 500 million, with continuing increases projected through the twenty-first century.

In communities all across the United States, people are already grappling with increasing traffic congestion, a shortage of landfill space and worsening air and water quality—all problems to which population growth makes a significant, if not exclusive, contribution. Their children could end their lives in a country twice as crowded and probably more polluted than it is now.

Elsewhere, the effects of rapid population growth are far more severe. In the developing world, population growth has magnified the adverse effects of bad government policies and social inequities, contributing to extensive deforestation, land degradation, overcropping, urban over-crowding and worrisome political trends. Among the wealthy industrial nations of Europe, meanwhile, population growth underlies significant new social tensions and the growth of pernicious right-wing political movements. The cause: a continuing flow of humanity across the Mediterranean in search of the jobs that North Africa's inefficient economies are unable to generate fast enough to keep up with population growth.

The region with the world's lowest population growth is bracing itself for worse to come from the region with the world's highest. Africa, which today has about as many inhabitants as Europe, will have three times Europe's population within a generation. Europe's immigration laws are already tightening as millions of dispossessed Africans are knocking on its doors. In the future, national budgets in Europe will be stretched to provide the resource transfers needed to help African nations provide for their own. The implied threat to European nations, explains the Rand Corporation's Marten Van Heuven, is that "either you visit the problem where it is or the problem will visit you." If a blowup occurs or if Islamic fundamentalists take control of a country like Algeria, a million or more refugees, including European expatriates, could head for Europe seeking asylum, according to European estimates.

Threat to Global Security

Population issues should command the attention of the public and policymakers for another reason: Demographic change is contributing to political and social dislocations that could put the most serious strains on the international system in the post-cold-war era.

Rapid population growth can affect security in various ways. In rural settings, competition for land, intensified by rapid population growth, could be a catalyst of conflict between large landholders and impoverished peasants. In urban areas the combination of crowded conditions, pollution, crime, lack of sanitation and shortages of public services, and the frustration of expectations raised by broader exposure to the media, produce a considerable potential for violent upheaval, according to one group of scholars who recently reported on the implications of demographic trends for U.S. security.

Throughout the developing world, meanwhile, governments are struggling to counteract the downward tow exerted by rapid population growth on domestic economies and, in particular, on the potential for job creation. Some 500 million people in the Third World are already

17

un- or underemployed, and 30 million more are entering the job market each year, according to the United Nations Population Fund (Unfpa). By the International Labor Organization's calculations, 350 million jobs will have to be created in less-developed countries during the 1990s alone.

Many experts doubt that capital and technology can be created fast enough in poor countries to keep up with the demand. If they are correct, welfare costs and political discontent could escalate. Simultaneously, authoritarian rule could be imposed or strengthened as governments, hard pressed to provide the health, housing, employment and education needs of swelling populations, seek to retain control. As one political leader, quoted in the UN publication *Populi*, warns, in Mexico, a country that particularly worries U.S. policymakers, "The consequences of not creating [at least] 15 million jobs in the next 15 years are unthinkable. The youths who do not find them will have only three options: the United States, the streets or revolution."

Rapid population growth can have other important, if less direct, consequences when it is linked to competition for scarce resources. In 1990 the American Academy of Arts and Sciences in Cambridge, Massachusetts, and the University of Toronto's Peace and Conflict Studies Program assembled a group of 30 experts to evaluate the connection between environmental degradation and conflict. The panel reported that deteriorating environmental conditions, which are partly the result of population pressures, have already contributed to dislocations and violent conflicts in many parts of the Third World. Unless broad social, economic and technical reforms are instituted in time, the panel concluded, such conflicts could foreshadow an upsurge of violence induced or aggravated by environmental decline.

In the worst case, such violence could take the form of interstate strife. The most serious threat concerns control of rivers and watersheds. Experts predict that the intensification of competition for diminishing water supplies in regions like the Middle East, fueled in part by rapid population growth, will lead to either unprecedented cooperation or lethal conflict. Conflict could also result as millions of "environmental refugees" abandon over-worked, worn-out land in search of a better life. In one troubling precedent, population pressures have prompted

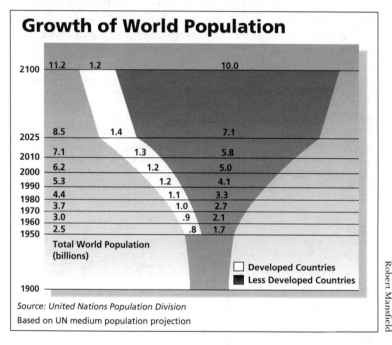

Growth of World Population

Year	Total	Developed	Less Developed
2100	11.2	1.2	10.0
2025	8.5	1.4	7.1
2010	7.1	1.3	5.8
2000	6.2	1.2	5.0
1990	5.3	1.2	4.1
1980	4.4	1.1	3.3
1970	3.7	1.0	2.7
1960	3.0	.9	2.1
1950	2.5	.8	1.7

Total World Population
(billions)

□ Developed Countries
■ Less Developed Countries

Robert Mansfield

Source: United Nations Population Division
Based on UN medium population projection

an estimated 10 million Bengalis to quit Bangladesh since the 1970s and to migrate to the Indian states of Assam and Tripura, with their more favorable growing conditions. This surge of humanity has disrupted landholding patterns and economic relationships and engendered ethnic conflict. (For additional information about the panel's findings, see *Headline Series* No. 300, "Environmental Scarcity and Global Security," by Thomas F. Homer-Dixon.)

Experts agree that coping with the threats posed by rapid population growth, among other factors, will require a radical restructuring of American foreign policy, away from the unilateralism of the cold-war era and toward closer coordination with the Western industrial democracies. In lieu of containing and deterring the Soviet Union, U.S. policy will have to be dedicated to careful monitoring of environmental and economic conditions around the developing world. The United States will also have to harness its multibillion-dollar intelligence capability to the task of providing early warning of regional conflicts and military applications of high technology by small countries. The United States and its Western allies will also have to be more attentive to inequities in the international economic system that exacerbate population-induced instability, perhaps channeling more foreign investment to the Third World, reconfiguring overseas development assistance and equalizing the terms of trade between rich and poor nations.

"In the end we're going to have to take equity very seriously," says Brookings Institution scholar John Steinbruner. "One way to do that is with a macroeconomic policy that succeeds in getting the globalizing economy to extend rather than restrict the participation of poor nations."

Given the technological achievements of the past two centuries, as well as the grim, mostly localized examples of the contribution rapid population growth has made to poverty and environmental decay, it is hardly surprising that experts view the future through radically different lenses. The optimists, endowed with faith in science, technology and the free market, see open-ended possibilities for mankind. The most extreme pessimists foretell demographically driven privation, environmental overkill and economic collapse. In fact, both futures are possible.

The experts who worry that the population bomb has not fizzled have a point. When people began talking about the population explosion 25 years ago, the world was growing by 50 million people every year. Today the annual addition is nearly twice that number and still increasing, despite lower rates of population growth. If birthrates decline no faster in the future than they did in the 1980s, the world will at least triple in size before population is stabilized. Few could gainsay that such growth poses an unprecedented challenge to mankind.

The experts who herald mankind's past achievements and perpetual ingenuity have a point as well. Despite unprecedented increases in population growth, the world is better off in many quantitative respects, if not always in terms of quality of life. In the aggregate, if not in some individual countries, infant mortality is lower, literacy rates are higher and prosperity is more widespread. It is true, meanwhile, that the pressures of rapid population growth have sometimes been the mother of invention, spurring scientists and engineers to come up with solutions to the very problems such growth has created. It is true as well that smarter government policies could go far toward alleviating the effects of rapid population growth.

One thesis of this book is that the future does not *have* to be one of population-induced scarcity and environmental decline but that it *may* be, and for the very reason that the soundly conceived and efficiently implemented policies needed to redeem the future are in such short supply in the countries that need them most.

Rx: Do 'Most Things Right Most of the Time'

The task of accommodating the kind of population growth expected in dozens of the world's poorest countries would tax the capacities of even the richest. Without the benefit of prosperity, the crucial requirement will be to do "most things right most of the time," according to one UN study. But as the same study suggests, hundreds of case studies, including those cited in these pages, serve "to give warning rather than inspire hope." In Egypt, urban housing for lower-income families is in short supply partly because of anachronistic rent-control laws. In Guatemala, forests are felled partly because of inequitable land distribution. In neither of these countries is population growth the main culprit. But in each case population growth has made the negative effects of short-sighted policies even more severe, and it will likely do so to a greater degree in the future.

Thus high political and institutional barriers separate what *can* be done to mitigate the effects of rapid population growth—implementing enlightened agricultural policies, for example—from what is likely to be done in all too many countries. As a team of population experts meeting in 1988 concluded: "Successfully meeting the challenges posed by rapid population growth . . . will require that technical and institutional adjustments be implemented and human and financial resources be mobilized at rates that are unprecedented in all of human history."

2

The Explosion of the Cities

When Napoleon Bonaparte led his legions into Egypt in 1798, the country's population was under 4 million. As late as the mid-1930s it was only 16 million. Then it doubled, and doubled again; now there are over 60 million Egyptians. About 13 million of them live in greater Cairo. To walk the streets of the city is to think they are all there in front of you, blocking the sidewalk with their old chairs, hawking produce or fish or whatever comes to hand.

Cairo is a city with a long history. It was founded over 1,000 years ago, after the Muslim conquest of Egypt. Since then it has been occupied by Turks, French and British. In terms of its influence in the Arab world, as Egyptian sociologist Saad Eddin Ibrahim notes, it is as important as Paris, the Vatican, Oxford, Hollywood and Detroit combined.

But today it is in danger of becoming a city of hard-pressed, hopeless men and women with no steady jobs and few prospects. Cairo's unremitting growth has created massive congestion, environmental degradation and poverty. It is a combustible mix that, in the opinion of some Egyptian experts, poses real risks of political and social collapse.

Cairo is just one example of the explosive urban growth that has led the world to the brink of a historic turning

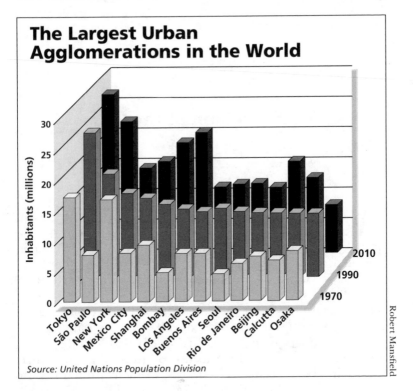

The Largest Urban Agglomerations in the World

Inhabitants (millions)

Tokyo, São Paulo, New York, Mexico City, Shanghai, Bombay, Los Angeles, Buenos Aires, Seoul, Rio de Janeiro, Beijing, Calcutta, Osaka

2010
1990
1970

Source: United Nations Population Division

Robert Mansfield

point. Demographers calculate that sometime around the turn of the century a majority of the world's population will be packed into urban areas like Cairo for the first time in human history.

The development is as sudden as it is dramatic. Cities first appeared 10,000 years ago, after the advent of herding and cropping made a sedentary, nonnomadic lifestyle possible. But they were few, far between, and, for the most part, small. Until modern times only one, Changan (now called Xian), the imperial city of the Tang Dynasty in China, ever reached a population of one million.

Next to population growth itself, the dominant demographic trend of the late twentieth century, according to the Worldwatch Institute, has been urbanization. As the authors of a survey of 100 urban areas concluded in 1988, the problems associated with this massive ingathering constitute "one of the great issues of humanity in the twentieth century." The speed of urban growth is suggested by a UN Development Program projection that between 1990 and 1995 alone, 320 million people—the equivalent of 18 cities the size of New York—will be added to the world's urban areas.

One extreme example of the relentless mathematics at work is greater Lagos, the capital of Nigeria, which now has a population of nearly 8 million. In 1950 Lagos had just 288,000 inhabitants. By century's end it will have 13.5 million. In 2010 it will have 21 million. Cities like São Paulo, Brazil, with 18 million now and swelling by half a million residents each year, do not lag far behind.

The astonishing speed with which megacities have grown has created megaproblems, for most urban governments have had neither the money nor the management and technical skills to keep pace. It took London 130 years to climb from 1 million to 8 million residents. Mexico City covered the same growth in just 30 years, between 1940 and 1970. Sixteen years later the city's population had doubled to 16 million. Faced with vast numbers of jobless and dispossessed, urban areas around the world, like Mexico City, are sagging under the weight of overwhelming demands for sanitation and water supplies, housing and employment, transport and public safety. Such problems prompted one city—São Paulo—to resort to an unusual tactic. In an effort to discourage more rural immigrants, it produced a series of TV spots bearing the message that life will be worse in the city.

Poignant evidence that urban governments are failing to keep up can be found in squatter communities that have sprung up in cemeteries in Cairo, garbage dumps in Mexico City, dry riverbeds in Karachi, Pakistan; in the tens of thousands of illegal, unsafe housing units that have cropped up in São Paulo; in the 4,000 tons of trash that accumulate daily in the Philippine capital, Manila; in the air pollution that has condemned 60 percent of Calcutta, India, residents to breathing disorders; in wastes that wash out of an overloaded sewage system onto the streets of Alexandria, Egypt; in the 20 million homeless—the equivalent of the combined populations of London and Paris—who wander the streets of Latin America's cities.

Most of all, poverty can be found in the shantytowns—lost cities or mushroom communities, as they are variously known—that have cropped up around the periphery of most Third World metropolises, cut off from roads, electricity, health services, clean water and sanitation. Half the populations of Delhi, India, Nairobi, Kenya, and Manila are slum dwellers. Slum rates are almost as high in Casablanca, Morocco, Calcutta, Bogotá, Colombia, and Kinshasa, Zaire, according to a 1990 Population Action International study that ranked cities according to 10 indicators, ranging from pollution to housing.

As Yale University historian Paul Kennedy notes in his book *Preparing for the Twenty-First Century*, the phenomenon of runaway urban growth in poor nations has changed the whole meaning of cities. For thousands of years, great urban centers like Rome and Paris, Vienna and London, have been associated with wealth and creativity, culture and economic opportunity. "By contrast," writes Kennedy, "Asian, Latin American and Central American megacities of 20 million inhabitants have become increasingly centers of poverty and social collapse."

The good news associated with this explosive urbanization is that it encourages smaller families. The bad news is that with population-doubling times in the Third World so

Cairo: People, Poverty and the 'New Islam'

Through the 1970s the Egyptian state was seen as a provider. Society seemed reasonably equitable. People had jobs; basic needs were met. Now the masses are beginning to feel that the state has broken the social contract. Many Cairenes no longer identify with a common cause or a sense of participation. As a result, say some Cairenes, the country is splitting into two institutions: the state, and the mass of people.

"In this climate it's not a surprise that even fanatics, if they care for the group—let's forget how illogical some of the teaching—have prospered," says Tahseen Basheer, a former Egyptian ambassador to Canada and the Arab League.

The signs of their prospering are evident in the vast social network that has sprung up outside official channels and which is paid for and controlled by Islamists. In many Cairo neighborhoods, Islamic schools, clinics and hospitals rival or substitute for their government counterparts.

"They are answering a need for social order and values because the government and society and the bourgeoisie no longer care," says Basheer. "In this context their role is not negative, even though you get a bag of nonsense with that good service. What the Islamic extremists are doing is creating a new family. They are creating self-support, even psychological support."

If the "new Islam" is a protest against the status quo, it is also the most visible expression of the fact that a vast new underclass has emerged in Cairo that has neither a stake in the society nor a disposition to abide by its rules. "I don't like terrorism," says Basheer. "But the terrorism and killings are signposts telling us of the danger."

The link between unemployment, hopelessness, desperation and fundamentalism seems clear.

"When you face problems that are beyond the scope of what you can deal with, you seek the refuge of religion," observes one Western diplomat in Cairo. "When you seek the refuge of religion you don't seek a moderate one. The fundamentalists are saying, work hard, be born again, you can go to heaven. They're offering something the state has long since ceased to offer: hope."

"So where does someone like this go?" asks Egyptian journalist Mohammed Auda in concurrence. "He goes to the mosque. He joins people who believe this is a society that must be destroyed because it can't be changed. And population is one of the main causes."

short, it will take a long time for the good news to have much of an impact. Until it does, national governments will have to face excruciatingly difficult choices as they seek to balance the needs of urban and rural populations.

The "urban bias" demonstrated in many poor nations has helped keep food prices low for city dwellers. But in the process it has depressed agricultural production, creating an expanded need for food imports, which have to be purchased at the expense of domestic economic development. Low farm prices have also forced farmers off the land and into the city, even as urban growth consumes valuable farmland. The result: As the need for food has grown, the capacity to produce it has diminished.

"There probably won't be a megacollapse because cities have built-in protective mechanisms," according to Saskia Sassen, an urban affairs specialist at Columbia University. "Some are institutional, like police and security systems. Some are geographical, like the citadels where the rich live. Some are ideological, like the promise of the good life that can be gained by staying within the law. It's like the mechanisms that were built into the financial system to deter a repetition of the 1929 crash."

A World Bank official issues a more apocalyptic prediction: "Urban poverty will become the most significant and politically explosive problem in the next century."

3

Feeding the World

When he received the Nobel prize in 1970 for his research leading to the Green Revolution, Norman Borlaug warned that the new technology would buy only a limited amount of breathing room—30 years at most—for governments to implement effective policies to slow population growth. But population growth did not decline fast enough, nor did investments in human resources—the medical care, education and nutrition needed to keep farmers healthy and productive—rise fast enough during the 1970s and 1980s to provide a cushion against food shortages in dozens of Third World nations.

"Those two things have come too slowly. That's why we're still in a mess," says Joachim Von Braun of the International Food Policy Research Institute in Washington, D.C., who notes that within a decade countries like Kenya and Rwanda could have two and a half times as many mouths to feed as in 1980.

One possible answer to the problem of continuing

localized food shortages is to do what farmers have historically done to raise output: expand the total acreage under cultivation. Right now about 11 percent of the earth's land surface is under cultivation.

Just how much new land is available for cultivation is difficult to calculate. At one extreme are the estimates of the Hudson Institute's Dennis Avery, who calculates that the development of acid-tolerant seeds now makes it possible to convert up to one billion acres of acidic savannah land into high-yield acreage that could also support large cattle herds. Avery points to another half-billion acres of inland wetlands in Africa that could be fitted with dams and dikes to produce high-yielding wet rice.

"If we brought back the 60 million acres of diverted cropland in the United States and cultivated the pampas [of South America] at their full potential, 1.5 billion more people could be fed," says Avery.

At the other extreme are the estimates of the Worldwatch Institute, which says that most of the potentially cultivable land is now being farmed and warns of the environmental consequences of exploiting the kind of marginal lands—including Africa's wetlands—that remain.

FAO Projects Doubling of Farmland

The most widely cited estimates have been issued by the UN's Food and Agriculture Organization (FAO), which in 1988 calculated the world's potential arable land to be just over 2 billion hectares (close to 5 billion acres), a 40 percent increase over today's usage. With significant drainage and irrigation, farmland could double worldwide, according to the UN agency.

If the FAO's calculations are correct, the expansion of cropland alone—in theory, at least—could keep food production rising as fast as the UN's medium population projections through the mid-twenty-first century. In fact, the estimates may be somewhat misleading, partly because of the added costs that would be required to bring marginal land under cultivation. As a result, only a small part of the surplus cultivable land in developing countries is likely to be tapped by the end of the decade, the UN agency estimates.

Most of the surplus land lies in regions of irregular rainfall. Costly irrigation projects would therefore be required to bring two thirds of the FAO's estimated surplus area under cultivation.

Predicting how much more land can be brought under cultivation is complicated by two other factors. One is the speed with which land is losing agricultural value due to erosion. The FAO calculates that a fertile area the size of the island of Ireland is being lost to erosion each year, the length of time it takes to add 100 million to the world population.

The other factor is the value of alternative uses. In theory, Kenya, for example, could turn game parks into cropland. But the income produced by tourism, the country's largest source of revenue, far outweighs the potential benefits of increased food production. Other governments have to calculate the consequences of felling valuable tropical and hardwood forests to create farmland that, while helping alleviate poverty in the short term, may be only marginally productive over the long term.

Even if most of the potentially cultivable land were not too wet or too dry, too saline or too acidic to be brought under cultivation cheaply, the problem of maldistribution remains. Vast surpluses exist in countries like Brazil and Argentina, where up to 80 million acres of the pampas await cultivation. But countries in which population pressures are greatest are not so favored. In 1988, 95 percent of potentially cultivable acres in Asia, including nations with high birthrates like India, Pakistan and Bangladesh, were already under cultivation, according to the FAO. In the Near East and North Africa, virtually all suitable and partly suitable land is under cultivation.

The situation is better in sub-Saharan Africa, where only

18 of 37 countries will be using more than half their farmable land by the end of the century. But even here usable land is irregularly distributed. Zaire and Zambia, for example, have large reserves. Rwanda, for one, has none, which means that however much new land is brought under the plow worldwide, only higher food-import bills await at home. The crucial consideration, therefore, is whether the distribution of land resources coincides with the distribution of people. In most countries it does not, which is one reason that new land alone may not be a major factor in expanding agricultural production. Another reason is that water supplies don't always exist where the available land exists. What's left once the unlikely is subtracted from the possible in terms of added land use is difficult for experts to say. Some gains are possible but not without high investments, accelerated deforestation and land degradation. Even at such cost, new land alone is not likely to be the key to long-term global food security.

The most promising—some say the most worrisome—possibility for expanding food production emerged in 1973, when two California scientists, geneticist Stanley N. Cohen of Stanford University and biochemist Herbert W. Boyer of the University of California, San Francisco, announced the discovery of a new technology called recombinant DNA.

Using molecular "scissors" known as restriction enzymes, the two took genes from the chromosomes of a toad cell and inserted them into a plasmid, a tiny packet of DNA that could introduce genetic information into foreign bacteria. When the bacteria reproduced, they reproduced the toad genes as well, creating a new type of bacteria. The experiment a success, evolution suddenly lost its monopoly over the power to produce new species.

Genetic Engineering Given Green Light

The gestation period of biotechnology ended in May 1992 when, after long deliberation, the U.S. Food and

Drug Administration ruled that gene engineering per se was not hazardous, that it would not require labeling on genetically altered food, and that it would leave the responsibility for food safety in the hands of producers.

Americans got their first taste of the incipient biotechnology revolution in the spring of 1994, when the first genetically altered food item—the Flavr Savr tomato—hit the market after two decades of research.

Other breakthroughs from splicing and transferring genes from one species to another are imminent: leaner, high-litter hogs; cereals that resist insects, diseases and herbicides; field crops engineered to retard the formation of ice during frosts; raspberries that last longer before spoiling; potatoes with less starch to improve frying; other food crops resistant to salt and drought. The list of possibilities appears endless.

Even skeptics are dazzled by the possibility that biotechnology could solve Africa's food crisis by making possible both the intensification and "extensification" of agricultural production. For example, genetically altered cassava and other food crops that could resist pests, diseases and weeds could make possible huge additional harvests on existing land. Crops that could grow in brackish soil, meanwhile, could expand onto millions of acres of unused land.

"If you could develop strains of crops that are much more tolerant to salt, then you could really potentially break open the ball game," acknowledges the Worldwatch Institute president, Lester Brown. "That would make an enormous difference."

Whether the "gene revolution" can produce the quantum leap in food output achieved by the Green Revolution has become a matter of intense debate. The potential of biotechnology, like that of the Green Revolution, is assessed in different ways by different people. Some say it will save millions from starvation. Others say it will merely expand the use of pesticides, lead to greater food import bills and hasten the decline of subsistence farming. The two views are not entirely incompatible.

At the most basic level, the debate between defenders and critics of biotechnology reduces to the propriety of changing rather than adapting to nature, of opting for human selection over natural selection. One battleground in the debate is the issue of whether biotechnology threatens sustainable agriculture. Critics worry that if researchers develop in wheat or corn crops the nitrogen-fixing properties of legumes, farmers might delete legumes from their repertoire of crops, eliminating nature's own mechanism for restoring nitrogen to plants.

If there is any consensus on this controversial issue it is that biotechnology has the potential—eventually—to make a significant contribution to increased agricultural output, first by enhancing the survivability of crops and only later by increasing crop yields by the more complex process of multiple gene transfers. But among most mainstream experts, hopes are tinged with realism.

Biotechnology is not likely to be a panacea. But as one part of a multiple strategy, it could play an important role in helping keep food production apace with population growth.

Paradoxically, the other key to global food security lies at the opposite end of the technology scale. It is to encourage low-technology, small-scale agriculture, especially in Africa.

Africa has the potential to be a productive continent. Its farmers are inventive and adaptable. It has 20 percent of the world's cultivable land but only 9 percent of its people, which translates into a third fewer people per acre than the developing world as a whole. But in most African countries, food production is not keeping up with population growth.

Most experts agree that the basic problem is that African governments neglect agriculture shamefully. It is a circumstance reinforced by the political impotence of small African farmers and rooted in what one U.S. Agency for

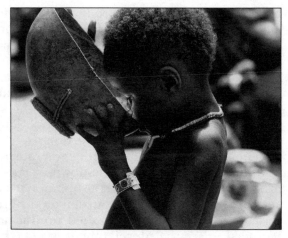

In war-torn southern Sudan, Unicef provides fortified milk where no food security exists. Even in peace, most African governments neglect agriculture.

International Development (AID) official, R. Stephen Brent, has described as the "fundamental conflict between the economic imperative of empowering the countryside and the antirural bias of African governments and skilled workers."

One needed measure is to provide security of land tenure, without which few farmers are likely to make the long-term investments, such as planting hedges and trees, that are needed to arrest soil erosion. Another needed measure is investment in rural infrastructure, including water and irrigation systems, bus and truck transportation, agricultural extension services and rural credit. The beneficial effects of such investments were demonstrated recently in Tanzania. A 1989 study showed that every $1.00 invested in transportation in this African nation yielded $1.50 in increased income, in part because new roads gave farmers confidence that their goods could get to market.

A third reform needed to spur small-scale agriculture in Africa is an adjustment of policies that favor large commercial farms at the expense of smallholders.

African nations also need to do more to assist women, who may be the key to Africa's food future. Eighty-five percent of rural women produce 80 percent of Africa's food, but because of laws and policies that discriminate against women, less than 10 percent of them own land or resources.

Idriss Jazairy is the former president of the International Fund for Agricultural Development, a small UN agency that deals with rural poverty. He says the key to Africa's food future is the very small farmer so long ignored by African governments and outside donors.

"The failure of past development strategies is that they have been based on a trickle-down, social-safety-net approach that emphasizes the consumption needs of the poor and identifies the poor as a burden on the growth process. Instead, we need to focus on their producing possibilities. We need to see that development is something that happens because of the poor, not in spite of the poor."

4

Models of Family Planning

Across most of the developing world, a quiet revolution is taking place that marks the beginning of the end of an era of unprecedented population growth. Using new technologies and innovative advertising campaigns, countries like Thailand and hundreds of private family-planning organizations around the world have begun tapping into a sizable latent desire for small families. The result, a sharp increase in the use of contraceptives and a corresponding decrease in the size of the average family, has far surpassed the expectations of population experts. A dramatic success story, it is perhaps the most significant single development of the post-World War II era.

A period of declining birthrates began during the 1960s and 1970s, when leaders of many less-developed nations first grasped the implications of rapid population growth for economic development and living standards. Armed with two revolutionary new contraceptives, the birth control pill and the intrauterine device (IUD), dozens of fledgling public and private family-planning agencies sallied forth with an equally revolutionary message: Family size is a matter of choice, not fate.

The revolution in contraceptive practice has reached into nearly every corner of the globe, slicing across continental lines and transcending religious and cultural barriers. Fertility declines have been sharpest in East Asia, where a combination of strong voluntary family-planning programs and rapid economic growth has lowered the average family size in South Korea, Taiwan, Singapore and Thailand to near or below replacement level. China has matched that accomplishment largely through aggressive, sometimes coercive measures to limit family size. Significant fertility declines have also been posted in Latin America, where Cuba has led the way, as Population Reference Bureau president Peter Donaldson notes, by taking the "sting from leftist charges that family planning was Western imperialism in disguise."

Largely excluded from the trend toward lower fertility has been sub-Saharan Africa, where women still bear an average of more than six children and where, in most countries, fewer than 10 percent of married women are using modern contraceptives. But even in Africa there are heartening exceptions. In Botswana and Zimbabwe, where national leaders have taken an active interest in limiting population growth, the use of contraceptives has increased significantly over the past 15 years. Under different social and cultural conditions, nations in North Africa have performed even better. In Morocco, for example, where mobile teams of nurses and midwives bring contraceptives to every doorstep, women now average 4.5 children, down from 6.9 in 1980. Even Kenya, once known for the world's highest birthrate, has experienced one of the more rapid fertility declines on record.

Only six countries, including Iraq and Saudi Arabia, are still dedicated to pronatalist policies that keep birthrates high and contraceptive use low. But these six are merely exceptions to a trend that, as the nonprofit Washington D.C.-based Population Institute's Werner Fornos suggests, has achieved a kind of critical mass worldwide.

"The transformation of perceptions about family planning . . . is all but complete," says Fornos. "Experience, circumstances and time have established a developing-world consensus that population must be brought into balance with resources and the environment. The consensus marks perhaps the first major milestone in the struggle toward population stabilization."

Where family-planning programs exist, there is evidence to show that they have made a significant and direct contribution to improving child and maternal health, protecting the environment, preserving finite natural resources and enhancing economic opportunities for users. Moreover, as the Rockefeller Foundation's Steven Sinding notes, the contraceptive revolution has been "as impressive as agriculture's Green Revolution and perhaps equally important in averting widespread famine in many developing countries."

Thailand: Pacesetter in Stabilizing Population Growth

One of the best examples of a family-planning success story is Thailand, where the transition from high to stable population growth has been attained in just over two decades.

A number of auspicious factors have played a role in Thailand's success. Distributing contraceptives to remote rural areas has been relatively easy in Thailand because it is a flat country with a good road system, much of it constructed by the United States during the Vietnam War. Communicating the family-planning message has also been relatively easy because nearly everyone in Thailand speaks the same language and adheres to the same religious faith, Buddhism.

The Thai government concluded that lowering the

population growth rate would enhance the prosperity of the nation. For their part, individual Thais concluded that having fewer children would enhance the prosperity of the family. The government's reasoning prompted it to begin providing contraceptive services. The reasoning of millions of Thai couples prompted them to accept such services with alacrity. When supply and demand came together, starting in the mid-1970s, fertility in Thailand plummeted.

That millions of Thais suddenly want smaller families is explained by two sweeping and simultaneous developments. One is the spread of the cash economy as the market system has penetrated into rural Thailand. The result has been the "monetization" of daily life. Many villagers have come to rely more on durable goods and specialized food items produced outside the home and advertised on the radios found in almost every rural hut. As John Knodel, a leading expert on Thailand, notes, most Thais are probably healthier, better fed, better educated and better clothed now than ever before. But dependence on the market has created a sense that, financially at least, life is more precarious and children more burdensome.

The other development is the extent to which population growth has outpaced the expansion of farmland in rural Thailand. With diminishing land for succeeding generations to inherit, parents have begun preparing their children for the salaried jobs in factories and cities that will provide higher incomes—enough higher that children will be able to support their parents in their old age. And that has meant education—where possible, all the way through secondary school.

Before family-planning programs were even begun, large numbers of people in countries like Thailand had already become aware of the incompatibility of large families and aspirations for a better life. That awareness meant that family-planning programs could make considerable gains just by tapping into the demand that already existed, even among the poorest rural women.

The longer explanation for why family-planning programs have been successful has to do with the various strategies they have employed to turn such latent demand into active demand—that is, how family-planning programs have helped translate new attitudes about family size into the concrete behavior reflected in the dramatic world-wide increase in contraceptive use.

Role of Government Leadership

Most of the world's 100-odd family-planning programs were launched from the top, as in Thailand, where services have since been decentralized. In Zimbabwe, for example, President Robert Mugabe briefly placed his sister-in-law in charge of a program that is now recognized as one of Africa's best. Bangladesh, a surprise success story, has been helped by consistent bipartisan political support.

National leadership is most important in countries where the authority of the central government effectively extends down through the political hierarchy to the local level. On the other hand, the extreme case of China, which has 22 percent of the world's population, demonstrates the hazards of overzealous national leadership. As late as 1974, the Beijing government, adhering to Karl Marx's notion that socialism could accommodate high fertility, pronounced population growth a "very good thing." Within four years, however, government leaders reversed themselves. Responding to successive postwar baby booms and fears of massive starvation, they threw their weight behind family-planning efforts begun in the 1960s, set rigid demographic targets, and in 1979 launched a campaign to limit Chinese couples to one child each.

Miguel Trias, president of Profamilia, the highly successful International Planned Parenthood Federation (IPPF) affiliate in Colombia, defines six characteristics of successful programs. "Curiously enough," he says, "each quality starts with the letter *a*": availability (timewise); accessibility (locationwise); acceptability (culturewise); affordability (moneywise); agreeability (pleasurewise); and appropriateness (healthwise). In Thailand and other countries with successful programs, most of these requirements have been met through the provision of locally oriented family-planning services designed to reach people who are uneducated, immobile and fearful or suspicious of using modern contraceptives. Most Thais do not have to travel farther than 2.5 kilometers or longer than 30 minutes to obtain basic family services, parameters that researchers have discovered are essential to success. Big drop-offs in the use of contraceptives occur when women have to invest more time and traverse greater distances to get them.

The open secret of Thailand's success is accounted for by additional factors common to other well-established family-planning programs. One is providing a broad range of contraceptives. Adding one new method to an established family-planning program increases the acceptance rate by as much as 12 percent and the chances of sustained contraceptive use. Those countries in which programs offer six or seven different methods have reached a much higher prevalence rate than those in which only three or four are offered, a UN study found.

Family planning in Thailand has also prospered because the government has harnessed the broadcast media to make the case for having smaller families and to promote the use of contraceptives. The use of media outlets in other countries confirms that radio and television can have a significant impact on reshaping values and creating demand for contraceptives. In Turkey, for example, awareness of family planning increased from 69 to 86 percent and contraceptive use rose from 39 to 42 percent as the result of one three-month mass media campaign.

One other key to the success of family-planning programs is sensitivity to the needs of clients, like the one who told a researcher in Honduras: "There should be more understanding for us humble people, because we go [to family-planning clinics] with fear." "In areas where people

In Bangladesh, women are taught safe delivery practices to help ensure healthy mothers and newborns.

are hesitant to practice contraception, the key to success is the warm and supportive attitude of the family-planning workers more than the type of contraception delivered," writes Australian National University demographer John Caldwell.

Sensitivity also extends to the realm of culture. In Africa, where large families have been a tradition, successful programs like Zimbabwe's have emphasized the need to space children to protect the health of the mother rather than limit family size. Latin American programs have made the same distinction to sidestep religious sensitivities.

Overall, the cost of providing family-planning services is surprisingly low, especially if administered as part of an existing health-care system. According to UN Population Fund figures, the average annual per user cost of family-planning programs in the developing world currently ranges between $10 and $25, though expanding the method mix will increase future costs. In India, where the program relies heavily on surgical sterilization, the amortized per capita cost is a mere $4.00. An expanding body of data suggests that this modest investment can pay big dividends.

A 1988 study in Mexico, for example, found that every peso spent by the Mexican social security system on family-planning services in urban areas between 1972 and 1984 saved nine pesos in reduced maternal and child costs. Two reasons cited were the number of unwanted births averted and consequently fewer incomplete abortions.

On a macroeconomic level, the UN Population Fund reports that of 82 developing countries it studied, the 41 with slower population growth managed to increase incomes by an average of 2.25 percent per year. In the 41 with faster population growth, incomes per person fell by an average of 1.25 percent per year. One official acknowledges that other factors besides low fertility contribute to strong economic performance. But, he says, "the coincidence between higher economic growth and lower population growth is no coincidence."

"A lot of governments are now in favor of family planning because they're looking at the issue from the standpoint of the obligations a country will acquire in the future by having high fertility: more schools, roads, hospitals, general services and housing," says Martin Vaessen, who has directed national surveys of reproductive behavior in developing countries for the Columbia, Maryland, firm of Macro International.

"People are slow to think through the implications of population growth until it translates into something they can understand, like traffic congestion or unemployment," concurs the former chief of U.S. AID's population program, Duff Gillespie.

Between the family-planning failures and success stories there is a third category of nations. Scattered mostly through Latin America and Asia, they have all made significant strides toward the goal of replacement fertility. But in each the pace of fertility decline has diminished since the early 1980s. In a few, including Indonesia and Tunisia, fertility actually stalled or plateaued for a time before resuming a gradual downward course.

Family-Planning Services Fall Far Short of Demand

One reason for the slowdown is that family-planning programs have run out of the easiest targets: people who had a strong desire for contraceptive services to begin with, for example, or who lived near family-planning clinics. As the programs have matured, it has been harder to sustain the kind of success they enjoyed early on.

Nearly all experts agree that one major requirement for stabilizing the world's population will be to increase the proportion of couples using contraceptives to roughly 75 percent—which means increasing the actual number of users by nearly 300 million—by the year 2000.

If the immediate unmet need for family-planning services could be satisfied, contraceptive prevalence in developing countries would rise to about 60 percent, a level that would lower average family size to just under three children per couple. But meeting the need will be a tall order. Only 60 percent of all women in the developing world have access to family-planning services. And even though the use of contraceptives in developing countries has soared since 1960, the total number of women not using any form of contraception—over 350 million—has declined only slightly because of the large increase in the numbers of women and men of reproductive age.

Meeting the demand for family-planning services will require 44 billion condoms, 9 billion cycles of oral contraceptives, 150 million sterilizations, and 310 million IUDs or Norplant insertions, to be exact, according to the Population Resource Center in Princeton, New Jersey. It will also require money—and lots of it.

One obvious way for developing nations to get the

money is for outside donors to give it to them. Right now foreign donors pick up less than a fourth of the almost $5 billion annual tab for family-planning services, which amounts to about 1 percent of total overseas development assistance.

One other way to help pay the bill is for the governments of developing countries to transfer some of the cost of family-planning services to the private sector, where perhaps 20 percent of couples now turn for contraceptives. A small percentage of upscale users around the world obtain contraceptives from the for-profit commercial sector. Even in poor countries, some upper-middle-class women buy at regular commercial outlets because of the appeal of using the best imported products. Millions of other couples concentrated in about 30 countries purchase subsidized contraceptives that are offered at lower prices through

Literacy class in Bamako, Mali. Education and job opportunities for women tend to lead to smaller families.

so-called contraceptive social-marketing programs, usually referred to as CSM. CSM programs rely on extensive commercial advertising and thousands of private outlets, from kiosks and convenience stores in India, to hairdressers in the Dominican Republic who sell government-donated condoms for a small profit, to village peddlers in Africa who now include condoms with their normal offerings of beer and cigarettes.

Men—A Neglected Target

Men, according to one prominent family-planning advocate, Malcolm Potts, are "the forgotten 50 percent of family planning." Men have largely been neglected because, absent the development of a male counterpart to the birth control pill, female fertility is still easier to regulate. But new circumstances have drawn attention to the role of men in the global movement to lower birthrates. One is AIDS, which has led to the promotion of condoms around the world. Another is progress in women's rights in the developing world, which has prompted more discussion of family planning in the household. A third is the advent of the no-scalpel vasectomy, pioneered in China, which obviates the need for incisions and stitches and has thus made the procedure more acceptable to men.

Research suggests that in many or most countries, male attitudes are not a major barrier to family planning. In countries where they have been, like Mexico and Nigeria, there is evidence that resistance is diminishing. Ninety percent of men say they are not opposed to family planning. But over 50 percent of women who are not participating in family planning say they are not doing so because their husbands are opposed. Fear that the use of contraceptives will provoke physical abuse is so strong in some regions that millions of women select methods that don't require the participation or knowledge of a male partner, like the pill or injectable hormones.

Beyond meeting the unmet need for contraceptives and

reaching hard-to-reach constituencies, bridging the gap to replacement fertility may require another, more controversial step: providing universal access to safe and inexpensive abortion services as a fall-back in case of contraceptive failure. Safe abortion relates most directly to the issue of maternal health: Where abortion is unavailable, illegal or prohibitively expensive, often unsafe abortions proliferate, leading to higher rates of maternal mortality. But the existence of legal, or at least widely available and safe, abortion services also has important demographic implications. Research compiled by the Population Council indicates that abortion has contributed to, without being indispensable to, fertility declines in every region.

"There will always be abortion," says Population Action International's president, J. Joseph Speidel. "The question is whether it will be a substitute for or a backup for family planning. If it's a substitute there will be a lot more of it because there will be a lot more unintended pregnancies."

The good news is that in many countries the definition of what constitutes ideal family size is already evolving downward. Part of the reason is broad social and economic forces like urbanization and modernization. But family size preferences can also be nudged downward by the day-to-day policy decisions governments make, like the decision to invest more money in education for girls or to create more economic opportunities for women. Expanding access to education alone could delay marriage and childbearing by years, breaking the back of population momentum, some experts believe. Thus the education and empowerment of women will be a necessary part of any widespread drop to replacement fertility—as we will see in the next chapter.

5

Women's Education and Empowerment

A growing body of evidence demonstrates that improving the status of women is not only a prod to development but, like family planning itself, one key to reducing fertility. As one recent UN report notes, there is an important connection between a woman's productive role—which is affected by the improved health, education and economic opportunities that are the source of empowerment—and a woman's reproductive role.

An international movement to advance women's reproductive rights began taking shape after government agencies and august foundations started pumping money into research projects on women's issues starting in the late 1970s. It coalesced at the 1985 UN Conference on Women in Nairobi, Kenya. It reached critical mass at a UN conference on human rights in Vienna, Austria, in 1993, where it attracted media attention and gained a degree of international recognition. Today thousands of reproductive-rights and reproductive-health advocates are scattered around the world, linked by a computer network that they have used to share information, coordinate strategy and advocate a reframing of the debate over global population policy.

Women's groups complain that overstating the consequences of rapid population growth has created a crisis atmosphere in some countries that has led to human-rights violations in the name of controlling fertility. The extreme case is China, where measures to implement an aggressive one-child policy have led to forcible insertion of IUDs, mandatory sterilizations and forced abortions.

Particularly offensive to women's groups are financial incentives that reward doctors and family-planning workers in over two dozen countries according to the number of acceptors they recruit. Family-planning advocates insist that programs to encourage contraceptive use are legitimate, pointing to the advantages that accrue to families and society from reduced population pressures. Feminist groups say incentive schemes place a higher value on reducing population growth than on enabling women to decide whether and when to have children.

The other target of the feminist critique is Third World governments that place the whole burden of reducing population growth on family planning. While family planning addresses the need for contraceptive services, it is less relevant to the other critical part of the population problem: the continuing demand for large families in many poor countries. For many women, the only path to status and economic security lies in having many children. Pervasive gender bias reinforced by custom, law and government policies in dozens of nations has deprived women of the very resources, jobs and educational opportunities—in short, the very means of empowerment—needed to reduce their dependence on children.

"Programs that put demographic objectives ahead of women's rights have not only failed to alleviate pervasive economic and environmental problems," says Jodi Jacobson, director of the Health and Development Policy Project in Washington, D.C., "but by diminishing the status of women they have further perpetuated the very problem family-planning agencies have set out to solve. You can never help women out of the population trap unless you help them out of the poverty trap, and you will never help them out of the poverty trap until you take steps to equalize access to resources."

Radical Fringe

A small group of radical feminists actually opposes family planning altogether and denies the existence of a population problem. The Population Council's Cynthia Lloyd notes that at its extremes the debate catalyzed by the women's movement has been waged between "those who care more about getting fertility down than helping women, and those who care more about helping women than getting fertility down." More typical is the centrist view that recognizes the contribution family planning is making to the improvement of women's status. By reducing domestic burdens, family planning is a fundamental part of any definition of empowerment. And by helping to space and limit births, family-planning programs have made a demonstrable contribution to the health of both children and mothers, saving as many as a million women's lives over the past quarter century, according to some estimates.

The conventional wisdom is that if a woman can retain a fair share of her earnings, she will need, and therefore have, fewer children. But researchers like Lloyd are just beginning to understand the extent to which families absorb the fruits of women's labor and to which the burden of family responsibility is being shifted to income-earning mothers. The effect of both developments has been to blunt the effects of empowerment on fertility.

"For 20 years we pursued the issue of women in development without looking at women in the context of their families," says Lloyd. "There's a growing concern that factors that have not been fully examined yet could attenuate the gains of empowerment."

The pattern identified by the Population Council's Susan

Greenhalgh in research in Ghana, India and Thailand is that men have reaped the surplus from women's entrepreneurship, either directly for themselves or indirectly in the form of reduced obligations to other family members.

"We've assumed that as the cost of children rises, the demand for children falls," comments Lloyd. "But that's only true if the person in control of decisionmaking is also the person who bears the rising costs. If the income comes home and gets co-opted away, then it doesn't have the kind of impact we hoped it would have."

"If men's family responsibilities are reduced, women will be left where they were before: dependent on men for essential resources and dependent on children for long-term economic security. Unless men are forced to bear parallel costs, what incentive do they have to cut fertility?"

Despite such findings, research still largely bears out the hopeful assumptions that the empowerment conferred by higher education and employment and buttressed by family-planning services does lead to lower fertility.

"The connection is clear and the rationale compelling: Fertility falls when women, or others who control them, can profit from a woman's work outside the agricultural sector or home," notes Virginia Abernethy, a professor of psychiatry at the Vanderbilt University Medical Center. "A woman with an independent income does not have to marry young or barter sex or childbearing for support."

In the biggest cities and remotest villages of the developing world, researchers have been quietly gathering new data to gain a better understanding of the factors that shape the motivation to have fewer children. Economic empowerment is clearly one. But empowerment has other dimensions that influence desired family size.

The most important by far is education, which, second only to access to good-quality family-planning services, has the most direct bearing on increased contraceptive use and lower fertility. One of the best examples of the relationship between education and fertility is the Indian state of

Kerala, where a female literacy rate of 87 percent has contributed to a fertility rate of 2.3, one of the lowest in the developing world. There are numerous other examples, including Sri Lanka, where female literacy and contraceptive prevalence have risen simultaneously to Western levels.

In recent years an old debate between advocates of the supply- and demand-side approaches to reducing population growth has given way to a strong and widening consensus that both family planning and social and economic development have strong independent effects on fertility and that the synergy between them is the most potent factor at work on high birthrates.

From this consensus a rough plan of action has emerged. The Population Council's Judith Bruce summarizes its main points: "that good family-planning services are important; that there are many deficiencies in quality that need to be improved; that the private sector and nongovernmental organizations need to be more involved; that men need more attention; that girls' education is important; that women need more access to resources; that family law has been neglected. In short, population policy should include more actions than it has in the past. It has to mean something more far-reaching."

But if the theoretical debate has been settled, the more practical question of where to invest limited resources to cope with high rates of population growth has not.

"As women get more power and more education, they acquire more modern concepts of life, including the idea of small families," summarizes Abbas Bhuiya of the International Center for Diarrheal Disease Research in Dhaka, Bangladesh. "It's as certain as the rising and the setting of the sun."

6

U.S. Policy
and the Global Agenda

Through most of his term as President (1953–61), Dwight D. Eisenhower thought population growth in Latin America and the newly independent nations of Africa and Asia was not a problem the United States needed to address. Advised to include family-planning assistance in U.S. foreign aid programs, he declined, saying he wanted to keep the government out of the bedroom.

Then, in the waning months of his presidency, he traveled to India. There he saw a poverty-wracked country that was growing by nearly 10 million people a year. He realized then that all plans for India's progress would fail unless measures to limit population growth were adopted. "It was people, people, and more people everywhere— people in such numbers, always increasing, that every plan and program for their betterment invariably set up goals too modest to assure progress as rapid as population growth," Eisenhower later wrote in his memoir, *Waging*

Peace. "My trip to India convinced me that we could not stand aloof if requested to help."

The evolution in Eisenhower's thinking mirrored that of the nation. In the early years of the cold war, assistance to limit population growth in developing nations was a sensitive political topic, opposed by conservative lawmakers and the Catholic Church. But from the early 1960s onward, the bad demographic news rolling out of the Third World made it clear that such aid was needed and that it would have to come from the rich, industrialized nations of the West.

Such a gradual awakening was also occurring at the UN, as the new international body acquired the technical expertise to measure and judge population changes. The UN's first step in this direction took place in 1946, when a Population Commission was established in the Secretariat to compile global demographic data.

The results of a comprehensive survey of postwar demographic trends in 1952 confirmed a growing suspicion: death rates were falling so fast in the developing world that it was on the verge of a period of unprecedented population growth.

Within the commission there were deep divisions about what to do about the data. The controversy was a microcosm of the struggles over population policy in Washington and at the UN that characterized the 20-year gestation period before the United States and the UN finally plunged into the business of providing technical and financial help to curb population growth.

Julia Henderson was then head of the UN's Bureau of Social Affairs, which included the commission, and the highest-ranking woman in the UN system. She describes the debate that grew hotter as the population figures soared higher.

"Some of the demographers [in the commission] said there's not much we can do about it. This is not an action group. We're here just to let people know what's happening. Others said the UN should be taking action to help developing countries deal with the population issue. There were lots of fights between the demographers and the statisticians. It went on for years before the tide turned."

Third World Countries Clamor for Family Planning

The tide turned in response to building pressure from the places that counted: the very Third World countries that were feeling the effects of rapid population growth the most and that most needed help. "The Indians kept coming and talking to me about how hard population was to deal with," recalls Henderson, who later served for 10 years as president of the International Planned Parenthood Federation. "They were saying we need help from the UN to organize and train our people to get family-planning programs going." But the tide turned slowly because of opposition from Catholic countries, some of which, like Argentina and Ireland, threatened to stop paying their dues if the world body actively promoted family planning.

While Catholic opposition was instrumental in keeping agencies like the World Health Organization and the United Nations Children's Fund (Unicef) out of family planning, support for a more activist population policy was gaining strength within the UN itself. One reason was the backing eventually provided by some of the former colonial powers, like Britain, which began to see what population growth was doing to retard development in their former domains in Africa and Asia. A turning point came in 1961 when France, which had staunchly opposed an activist role for the UN, made a huge tactical error.

"The French said they didn't think Third World countries really wanted assistance," Henderson remembers. "They said this was all generated within the UN. So they proposed that a questionnaire go out to all the countries to ask them: Did they have population problems? Would they welcome help from the outside? When the questionnaires all came back they overwhelmingly said yes, we have serious problems. Cities were beginning to explode. They didn't know what to do about health, jobs and education."

Within the developing world the only solid resistance came from African nations, newly freed from colonial rule and suspicious of the motives of the former colonial powers. But Asian nations pressed the case and were joined by several countries in Latin America, where urban growth was rapidly accelerating. By the mid-1960s many Third World nations had taken their second postwar census. The results confirmed that population growth had dramatically increased and helped to dispel much of the remaining resistance toward attempts to address it.

One final hurdle had to be cleared before the UN could embrace an activist policy. John F. Kennedy, a Catholic President (1961–63), was now in the White House. Of all postwar occupants of the Oval Office, he seemed least likely to countenance any change in U.S. population policy. As it happened, the population issue provided Kennedy with an ideal vehicle to redeem a campaign pledge not to be captive to the wishes of Rome.

Instructions were sent to the State Department to change U.S. policy by encouraging the UN to take a more active role in helping Third World nations to lower population growth rates. Within three years—by 1966—the General Assembly had passed a resolution authorizing UN agencies to respond to calls for help with technical and financial assistance to set up family-planning programs. Three years later the UN Fund for Population Activities—now called the UN Population Fund but still bearing the acronym Unfpa—was created. Not by accident, its first director was a Catholic—Rafael Salas, from the Philippines—who became an energetic cheerleader and fund-raiser on behalf of family planning.

The mood of the United States was not yet such that large sums could be voted for family planning. But in December 1963, shortly after Kennedy's assassination,

Congress, at the behest of Senator J. William Fulbright (D-Mo.), quietly passed legislation that approved government funds for research into population growth. At first things moved slowly. In fiscal 1964 the U.S. Agency for International Development made its first population-related grants: $100,000 for a Chilean demographic training center and $40,000 for a similar effort by the Pan American Health Organization. But agency officials were fully aware of the sensitivity of the population issue on Capitol Hill and prohibited any dissemination of manufactured contraceptives.

Then in 1965, three developments coalesced to push population higher on the AID agenda, as Phyllis T. Piotrow describes in her 1973 book, *World Population Crisis: The United States Response.* The first was political: At the urging of close advisers, President Lyndon B. Johnson (1963–69) referred to the population problem in his State of the Union address. The reference was only one sentence long and said simply that the United States would try to use its knowledge to help deal with the explosion in world numbers. But it was a more explicit endorsement of action than any White House had ever made, and activists seized on it as justification for their population work.

The second development was technological. By 1965 scientists had made great advances in contraceptive technology with birth control pills and the IUD. In the United States 4 million women were already taking the pill; IUDs were being adopted by Pakistan, India and other hard-pressed nations for their own population programs.

The third development was a disaster. A food shortage caused by bad weather, bad management and perhaps population growth hit many parts of the developing world in the summer of 1965. Monsoon rains failed in India, exacerbating the crisis. The President and Congress moved to provide emergency food aid—while urging attention to population as part of the solution. By the beginning of 1966, at least 15 countries had asked AID for help in starting population programs.

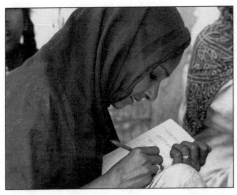

Indian woman learns to write in Unicef program to improve the status of girls and women.

© UNICEF/5858/Vilas

Between 1965 and 1980, the United States contributed roughly half of all international assistance for population and family planning. By 1990 the cumulative total of U.S. assistance had reached over $4 billion in aid, with about three quarters of that paying for actual family-planning services and the rest for research and policy development. AID became the world's largest donor of contraceptives.

"By promoting the availability and use of modern contraceptive techniques, AID helped slow the pace of population growth in the 1960s and 1970s," wrote *Washington Post* columnist Hobart Rowen. "It was one of our real foreign aid success stories, notably in Thailand, Indonesia, Mexico and Bangladesh."

One of the biggest threats to the incipient movement to address rapid population growth was a general antagonism felt by the nations hardest hit toward the nations attempting to help. Developing countries were dissatisfied with the maldistribution of global wealth resulting, in part, from the inequitable terms of trade that existed between the rich industrial North and the poor South.

Anti-Western feelings came to a head in 1974 when the UN convened an international conference in Bucharest, Romania, to address the population issue in the context of national and global development. The conference was beset by a deepening conviction among Third World delegates that nothing could be done about population until economic and social conditions were improved. The view was encapsulated in the catchphrase "development is the best contraceptive," which became the informal slogan of the conference. As the final document issued at Bucharest put it more formally, "the basis for an effective solution of the population problem is, above all, socioeconomic transformation."

Adding to the complications was the concerted opposition of two of the strangest bedfellows in global politics: the Catholic Church, which was intensely opposed to the propagation of family planning based on the use of modern contraceptives, and the Communist bloc, which was convinced that capitalism, not population, was the cause of underdevelopment.

Despite the conflicts, the proceedings at Bucharest represented an advance for the incipient global family-planning movement. After all the rhetoric was expended, the conferees got down to the business of drafting and adopting by acclamation a blueprint for action that embraced the very premises urged by the Western nations: that there is a negative effect of population growth on development; that governments should include strategies to curb population growth in their social and economic plans; that there was a need for international action to support such strategies; and that part of any solution to the problem was according more rights to women.

U.S. Motives Mixed

There was certainly an element of altruism in the U.S. commitment to the task of curbing global population growth. As a National Security Council member wrote in a staff memorandum in 1975: "If significant progress can be made in slowing population growth, the positive impact on growth of gross national product and per capita income will be significant."

But the United States was also motivated by self-interest,

as the same memorandum made clear: "Whatever may be done to guard against interruptions of supply and to develop domestic alternatives, the U.S. economy will require large and increasing amounts of minerals from abroad, especially from less-developed countries. That fact gives the U.S. enhanced interest in the political, economic and social stability of the supplying countries."

No policy is set in stone, even one that developed a consensus in the U.S. bureaucracy over two decades of work. By 1980 U.S. family-planning aid was vulnerable, in part because of its own success. Starting in the late 1960s, record high population growth rates (though not the number of people added to the world's population each year) began to decline. Advances in agricultural technology, notably the Green Revolution, appeared to avert the threat of famine in developing nations. Back home it was easy for Americans to make the assumption that the population bomb was just about defused. "There was a sense that if you got population programs growing, the problem would be solved, so nobody was concerned anymore," recalls a spokesman for one national environmental organization.

Perhaps more important, a number of influential economists who questioned traditional assumptions about the negative effects of population growth on development were receiving more and more attention as the 1980s began.

The election of Ronald Reagan to the presidency in 1980 cleared the way for a significant number of men and women with fundamentally different attitudes on the population issue to replace the occupants of senior government posts. They brought to their jobs two new and complementary perspectives that were destined to have a huge impact on global family-planning efforts.

One was a belief in the virtues of classic laissez-faire economics. When they thought about population growth at all, they discounted it as a factor in the development process. Poverty was not a result of population growth but of flawed economics, they believed. The other perspective was brought by a group of hard-core antiabortionists who sought to dissociate family planning from abortion and, in some cases, targeted all modern birth control methods as well. By the end of the first year of the Reagan presidency, notes former AID population official and Population Action International's President Speidel, disciples of both schools were scattered through the Administration "like raisins in a rice pudding."

United States Reverses Population Policy

The first clear signal that population programs were in jeopardy came within President Reagan's first year in office, when the Office of Management and Budget sought to cut off all support for population activities. The effort failed.

On another front, reluctant AID career officials were forced by senior Reagan appointees to open the door to fringe groups advocating "natural" birth control methods.

In all of this, Administration officials were pushed by an increasingly sophisticated lobby that drew on the support of New Right think tanks, Roman Catholics and Protestant fundamentalists. It championed conservative views on personal morality and women's rights and opposed the growing use of contraceptive sterilization. But its real raison d'être was opposition to abortion. The event that had catalyzed the movement was the Supreme Court's 1973 decision in the case of *Roe v. Wade* that legalized abortion. After failing to gain sufficient support for an amendment to the Constitution to ban abortion at home, even with an antiabortion President in the White House, the movement, led by groups like the National Right to Life Committee, the American Life League and Human Life International, turned to a riper opportunity: abortion abroad.

The gathering discontent of these critics with the international family-planning movement and with the abortions they said it was promoting came to a head on the eve of two major events in 1984. The first was the successor to Bucharest, a huge international conference on population and development scheduled for Mexico City at the end of July. The second was the Republican National Convention, scheduled for Houston, Texas, two weeks later.

White House officials agreed to appoint a prolife delegation to the Mexico conference and chose assistant secretary of state James L. Buckley, director of Radio Free Europe and a former senator and under secretary of state, to head it. In Mexico, Buckley reversed the working premise of the previous five U.S. Administrations by announcing that population growth was a "neutral" factor in development, helpful or harmful depending on the economic conditions existing in any given country. "The relationship between population growth and economic development is not a negative one," Buckley proclaimed. "Indeed, both in the American experience and in the economic history of most advanced nations, population growth has been an essential element in economic progress."

The other American surprise in Mexico was an announcement that in the future funds would be denied to any organizations that "support or actively promote abortion as a method of family planning." The announcement was to touch two organizations that stood at the very nerve center of the international family-planning network. One was the International Planned Parenthood Federation, which helped support 120 member programs and a quarter of whose budget was then being supplied by the United States. The other was Family Planning International Assistance, the international arm of Planned Parenthood and one of AID's largest grantees. The two organizations, which together funded a handful of programs that gave advice or referrals on abortion, were cut adrift from the American budget. Over the next several years, more than a dozen other U.S. family-planning organizations were forced to disavow abortion to avoid losing U.S. AID funding.

Ironically, the country whose population problem was so severe and whose support for family planning had carried so much weight in Mexico City was also the country that gave credibility in the eyes of many Americans to the Reagan Administration's decision to draw the line on abortion. In February 1984, just four months before the Mexico City conference, the public television program *Nova* broadcast a disturbing exposé of human-rights abuses in China, which ranged from mandatory sterilization and abortions to forced insertions of IUDs, all committed in the name of slowing the country's runaway population growth. In late 1983 the Chinese government replaced senior family-planning officials and softened directives to local cadres. But the reforms were obscured by another round of publicity in 1985 as *Nova* re-aired its program, and as other TV series, including CBS's *60 Minutes,* as well as newspapers, including *The Washington Post,* provided more unsettling accounts of Chinese practices. Soon after, Unfpa was denied funds by the Reagan Administration for participating in the management of the Chinese program.

One of the abiding ironies of the Mexico City conference is that by the time the United States had forfeited its own leadership role, the governments of the developing countries themselves had reached a kind of epiphany on the subject of population growth. They came to Mexico not as skeptics and critics, as they had come to Bucharest, but as converts to the notion that slower population growth could make some contribution to economic development.

As one commentator noted later: "Almost every country arrived in Mexico in favor of action against rapid [population] growth. Indeed, there was very little debate on the subject, but also, unfortunately, very little publicity. It was a consensus achieved without conflict, but unnoticed by the hordes of journalists there."

Another notable development of the 1980s was the extent to which other nations stepped forward to bridge the funding gap created when the Reagan Administration

Mauritanian woman learning to operate a computer in government project to teach women nontraditional skills.

© UNICEF/5745/
Lauren Goodsmith

curtailed support for Unfpa and IPPF. The Netherlands, Norway and Sweden made up most of the loss. One consequence is that today funding for Unfpa is at an all-time high. The Reagan policy also catapulted Congress into the spotlight, as lawmakers rushed to fill the fiscal breach, appropriating funding that in most years exceeded what the Administration had requested. By 1985 the budget for population activities was half again higher than at any time during the Carter Administration.

Despite such gains, the overall effect of the Reagan and Bush years was to arrest temporarily the momentum generated through the five previous Democratic and Republican Administrations. At home, despite budget increases voted by Congress, the Reagan policy introduced a discordant note into congressional deliberations, ending two decades of consensus on the subject. Abroad, the need for family-planning services was growing faster than U.S. aid. Population funding in constant dollars on a per capita basis—that is, per couple of reproductive age in the developing world—actually declined during the Reagan years to the levels of the early 1970s.

By the end of the Reagan years, moreover, the expenditures that were being made were being justified on a substantially narrower basis. Since its inception, the population program within U.S. AID had been devoted primarily, if not exclusively, to demographic goals. The architects of the policy were principally concerned about the effects that rapid growth would have on the economic development, quality of life and political stability of Third World nations and thus believed that using family-planning programs to help lower birthrates was in the best interests of rich and poor nations alike.

Under pressure from the right, such cosmic justifications were jettisoned during the Reagan Administration in favor of the narrower though still important goal of improving family welfare—in particular maternal and child health—through greater access to family planning. In addition, effective contraception was promoted to conservative politicians as a means to reduce reliance on abortion.

Abroad, the consequences of the Reagan Administration's attempts to undercut family planning were more severe than at home. Over the next few years Unfpa was forced to turn down funding requests for dozens of family-planning projects. The cuts hit hardest in Africa, where the family-planning movement was just beginning to gather momentum and where 13 programs that IPPF was on the verge of funding were put on hold.

"It did damage," says one World Bank official of the Reagan policy. "You go to Third World countries and talk to finance ministers about population and get a lukewarm reception because of what the United States was saying. For those countries that were sitting on the fence it was the difference between delaying and plunging ahead with family planning."

In the end it may be the lost opportunities that have mattered most. The 1980s were a decade during which considerable advances were possible because of the heightened awareness in developing nations of the benefits of smaller families. But few such advances occurred in the absence of American encouragement and funds.

There is a final twist to the Reagan and Bush years,

wholly unintended by those who helped frame the population policy of the era. Their objective was to lower the global abortion rate. Their strategy was to separate abortion from family planning by withholding money from family-planning organizations that funded or provided abortion services or even counseled on the subject. In fact, some experts believe the policy may have had the consequence of increasing the number of total abortions worldwide. The absence of adequate family-planning services makes unintended pregnancies more likely, and these in particular, experts say, often end in abortion.

Even in the years before Reagan and Bush altered U.S. population policy, the time was not ripe to move population issues to the top of the agenda. Although many environmentalists, in particular, believed population growth was the engine of ecological decline, it was too risky to elevate the issue against a backdrop of intensifying abortion politics at home.

"It was on everyone's intellectual radar screen but it was not on everyone's political radar screen. The issue was not a political highflier," recalls Douglas Costle, who served as administrator of the Environmental Protection Agency during the Carter Administration. "But now it can't be avoided. The best politics ultimately follows the facts, and in this case the facts are catching up with everyone."

Clinton Lifts Restrictions on Family-Planning Aid

With the election of Bill Clinton as President, population has become a priority political item. Within months of taking office, the Clinton Administration took steps that amounted to a total reversal of the restrictive policies of the Reagan and Bush Administrations. Just two days after his inauguration, Clinton revoked the Mexico City policy, lifting the restrictions that prohibited some family-planning organizations from receiving U.S. funding because of abortion-related activities. Within months, the money started flowing: $13.2 million to IPPF alone as part of a five-year, $75 million commitment by U.S. AID. In another significant move the Administration immediately increased funding for population activities to over half a billion dollars, then pledged to press for increases up to $1.2 billion by the year 2000—the American share of the total amount needed to make family-planning services available to every woman who wants them. The amount was estimated at $9 billion at a 1989 UN population conference in Amsterdam, the Netherlands, where the goal of universal availability was set. That figure has since been revised upward to about $11 billion, with additional increases in subsequent years, reflecting the slowing of progress toward that goal in the late 1980s and early 1990s.

The Reagan and Bush Administration officials struggled to portray population-assistance advocates as zealots with a faddish view, says Dr. Piotrow, who directs the Center for Communication Programs at the Johns Hopkins University School of Public Health. The effect was to raise doubts about the population issue as a serious matter of public policy. "What Clinton has done is to restore the legitimacy of the issue. There's been a total change in tone."

Global Agenda

There is no secret about what needs to be done to reduce global population growth. Economic development, which will help reduce the demand for large families, will be one important component of a comprehensive strategy to reduce fertility and further slow rates of population growth in developing countries like Mexico. Another will be narrowing the inequities between the sexes that are prevalent in many developing nations. As one journalist summarizes the requirements: "Emancipate women. Educate them. Help them space their pregnancies. Give their children health care. Allow them options beyond motherhood." The investment that promises the biggest short-term payoff is simply making sure that safe and effective family-planning methods are made universally available.

The simple truth is that rapid population growth is one of the few soluble problems in an otherwise complicated world. Four decades of experience with family planning have made it abundantly clear what programs and methods work best. The experience of family-planning agencies in countries from Thailand to Mexico has provided valuable, transferable lessons that are even now being incorporated into the practice of countries that were late to set up population programs. New contraceptive or abortion technologies, like the abortion drug RU-486, may make an eventual contribution to lower fertility. But even with existing methods, the task of attaining population stabilization is both affordable and achievable.

"Family planning is one thing we know how to do well, so let's get on with it and rejoice," says Malcolm Potts, who teaches public health at the University of California at Berkeley. "Just provide services in a respectful way, listen to what people want, provide good geographically, culturally and economically accessible services, and fertility falls. That's what the data show. If you give people access to contraceptives and abortion they practically stop having children."

As Potts notes, rapid population growth is no longer a problem looking for a solution but a solution looking for resources. It was the resources of the industrialized nations that helped lower death rates in the developing world half a century ago, contributing to the population explosion that has occurred there since. The idea of investing the modest resources now needed to lower birthrates has appealing symmetry. More to the point, such an investment would be the consummate act of enlightened self-interest on the part of wealthy nations which, in the absence of such support, will not long remain isolated from the daunting consequences of rapid global population growth.

Talking It Over

A Note for Students and Discussion Groups

This issue of the HEADLINE SERIES, like its predecessors, is published for every serious reader, specialized or not, who takes an interest in the subject. Many of our readers will be in classrooms, seminars or community discussion groups. Particularly with them in mind, we present below some discussion questions—suggested as a starting point only—and references for further reading.

Discussion Questions

Until about 1600, the world's population remained below 300 million, with births and deaths roughly in equilibrium. Thereafter the population began to grow, slowly at first, then very sharply after World War II. What were the major causes for the rapid increase in the rate of growth?

The issue of global population is highly controversial. Nevertheless, there is general agreement among experts that projected population growth must be slowed and that this requires effective family planning and development plans. Do you agree? Which should receive priority—family planning or development?

The author states that to be effective, family planning will require countries to provide, among other things, increased educational opportunities for girls. What is the relationship between education, notably for women, and rapid population growth?

Some developing countries have completed in a single generation a demographic transition that took the West a century to achieve. However, others, such as India, have faltered on the road to replacement fertility. What accounts for the success of some countries and the failure of others to slow population growth?

Which regions have the highest rates of population growth? How do high population growth rates affect urbanization? the demand for schools, housing and jobs? the decline of the environment? population dislocations and conflicts?

What impact does rapid population growth in developing countries have on Americans and on U.S. foreign policy?

"Rapid population growth is no longer a problem looking for a solution but a solution looking for resources," as one authority has written. What resources must the United States and other Western democracies mobilize?

READING LIST

Appleby, R. Scott, "Religious Fundamentalisms and Global Conflict." *Headline Series* No. 301. New York, Foreign Policy Association, April 1994.

Brown, Lester, et al., *State of the World, 1993: A Worldwatch Institute Report on Progress Toward a Sustainable Society.* New York, Norton, 1993.

Buvinic, Mayra, and Yudelman, Sally W., "Women, Poverty and Progress in the Third World." *Headline Series* No. 289. New York, Foreign Policy Association, Summer 1989.

Closing the Gender Gap: Educating Girls. Washington, D.C., Population Action International, 1994.

Conli, Shanti, and Speidel, J. Joseph, *Global Population Assistance: A Report Card of the Major Donors.* Washington, D.C., Population Action International, 1993.

Davis, Kingsley, and Bernstam, Mikhail, eds., *Resources, Environment, and Population: Present Knowledge, Future Options.* New York, Oxford University Press, 1991.

Dixon-Mueller, Ruth, *Population Policy and Women's Rights: Transforming Reproductive Choice.* Westport, Conn., Praeger, 1993.

Ehrlich, Paul R., and Ehrlich, Anne H., *The Population Explosion*. New York, Simon and Schuster, 1991.

Fisher, Julie, *The Road from Rio: Sustainable Development and the Non-governmental Movement in the Third World*. Westport, Conn., Praeger, 1993.

Gardner, Richard N., *Negotiating Survival: Four Priorities After Rio*. New York, Council on Foreign Relations Press, 1992.

Hardin, Garrett, *Living within Limits: Ecology, Economics, and the Population Taboo*. New York, Oxford University Press, 1993.

Homer-Dixon, Thomas F., "Environmental Scarcity and Global Security." *Headline Series* No. 300. New York, Foreign Policy Association, June 1993.

Jacobson, Jodi L., *Gender Bias: Roadblock to Sustainable Development*. Worldwatch Paper 110. Washington, D.C., Worldwatch Institute, September 1992.

Kennedy, Paul, *Preparing for the Twenty-First Century*. New York, Random House, 1994.

Meadows, Donella H., Meadows, Dennis L., and Randers, Jergen, *Beyond the Limits: Confronting Global Collapse, Envisioning a Sustainable Future*. Post Mills, Vt., Chelsea Green, 1992.

Meyers, Norman, and Simon, Julian, *Scarcity or Abundance?: A Debate on the Environment*. New York, Norton, 1994.

Piotrow, Phyllis T., "World Population: The Present and Future Crisis." *Headline Series* No. 251. New York, Foreign Policy Association, October 1980.

Ross, John A., and Frankenberg, Elizabeth, *Findings from Two Decades of Family Planning Research*. New York, The Population Council, 1993.

Schiffer, Robert L., *The Exploding City: An Unforgettable Journey Through Nine Great Cities*. New York, St. Martin's Press, 1989.

Unfpa (United Nations Population Fund), *The State of World Population 1993*. New York, Unfpa, 1993.

World Commission on Environment and Development (the Bruntland Commission), *Our Common Future*. New York, Oxford University Press, 1987.

World Resources 1994–95: A Guide to the Global Environment. New York, Oxford University Press, 1994.